AMERICA IN CRISIS

MORRIS CERULLO

SAVE AMERICA NOW!

Table Of Contents

Foreword 5

Chapter 1
One Nation, Under GOD 7

Chapter 2
Denying God and Persecuting Those Who Acknowledge Him 13

Chapter 3
The Prophecy 17

Chapter 4
How the Mighty Have Fallen 21

Chapter 5
What You Can Do Now 27

This book or parts thereof may not be reproduced
in any form without written permission
of Save America Now!

All scriptural references are from
The KJV Bible unless annotated otherwise.

Published by:

SAVE AMERICA NOW!

P.O. Box 85260 • San Diego, CA 92186-5260

(858) 560-9333

E-mail: contact@save-america-now.com
Website: www.save-america-now.com

SAVE AMERICA NOW

Copyright © 2003
Save America Now!
Published by
Save America Now San Diego, CA.
All Rights Reserved.
Printed in the United States of America.

Foreword

Friend, you can pick up any book from almost any ministry in America and get a teaching about the moral degradation of our society.

You can read about how the world is getting more and more worldly and how the truth of the Gospel is being denied on a regular basis.

All of that is true, and it's coming to pass because Bible prophecy said it would.

You can read about it from almost any ministry because it **is** happening, and it is worrisome.

So if you've picked up this book to read about that, you'll find yourself challenged instead by a perspective that isn't being covered often—you see there's a difference between a prophecy **scholar** and a prophet.

There is room for both in God's kingdom, and both have their roles to fulfill.

The prophecy scholar reads what's in the Bible, what God has predicted for the future, and he interprets it for the audience God has called him to reach.

The prophet hears the Word of God from His own mouth and relays that message to the audience God has called him to reach.

I have read my share of prophecy; I've read the Bible many times.

I have studied prophecy all my life, but I don't consider myself a prophecy scholar—I'm simply a man God uses to reveal truth to His people.

God's calling on me is intense: He has called me to hear the Word at His feet and reveal that Word to YOU, the audience He has called me to reach.

Contained in this book is a tremendous prophecy God has called me to reveal to you, something He has told me to tell you, and I want you to know beforehand that this is unlike any prophecy I have ever been called to reveal.

In 1989, God gave me a tremendous revelation that I later released in book form called, *"Five Waves and Five Crises."* In the book, I revealed five waves of the Holy Ghost and five incredible crises that would happen in the 1990's.

Then, in the late 1980's, the economy was rip-roaring along on the end of the Reagan Revolution. George Bush (the father, not the son) had ridden the wave of Reagan's economy to office, and the world was flying high on an economic rush.

But God gave me a specific warning to reveal in that book: a financial crash of unprecedented proportions was coming in the 1990's, and **everyone** would feel it.

Can I tell you something?

Christians—people who are supposed to be attuned to God—**laughed** at me when I released that book.

They *laughed* when the dot-com revolution pushed the Dow Jones average to its highest historical level.

But they weren't laughing when the dot-com bubble burst, after businesses found out that *someone* had to buy something for advertising revenue to keep coming into Web sites that didn't actually sell for profit.

When the bottom hit, unemployment began to rise and the economy began to take a nose-dive—just as God had led me to reveal.

I said all that to say this: the true test of a prophet is that what he says comes to pass.

God has made that very clear. He has made it clear that what He says is GOING to come to pass!

So as you read this little book, please understand that I'm not writing it to scare you, or to make you believe something just for the sake of believing it.

No; I have received the command to communicate this information directly from God, just for you, because you are part of the audience He has called me to reach.

Chapter 1
One Nation, Under GOD

Prayer Target One

Friends, we must humble ourselves and seek the face of Almighty God. Pray that America will turn from her wicked ways and return to the Lord.

If my people, which are called by my name, shall humble themselves, and pray, and seek my face, and turn from their wicked ways; then will I hear from heaven, and will forgive their sin, and will heal their land.

2 Chronicles 7:14

The Declaration of Independence is the founding document for the greatest nation in the history of the world.

Think about that for a second.

The United States of America is the greatest nation in the history of the world, both militarily and economically.

That's phenomenal for a nation that has been around just a little over 200 years.

The Declaration of Independence was the document that started it all—it was the document that served notice to the King of England (which then was the most powerful nation in the world) that the American colonies would no longer serve, and would no longer pay taxes to the monarchy without representation.

It was a document that declared human beings could all have a reasonable expectation of rights and privileges, and the government existed to protect and guard those rights, not to grant them.

Read what the Declaration says:

We hold these Truths to be self-evident, that all Men are created equal, that they **are endowed by their Creator** with certain unalienable Rights, that among these are Life, Liberty and the Pursuit of Happiness—That to secure these Rights, Governments are instituted among Men, deriving their just Powers from the Consent of the Governed, that whenever any Form of Government becomes destructive of these Ends, it is the Right of the People to alter or to abolish it, and to institute new Government, laying its Foundation on such Principles, and organizing its Powers in such Form, as to them shall seem most likely to effect their Safety and Happiness.

The most fundamental thing to understand about that statement, is that the writer of it, Thomas Jefferson, predicated all the rights of mankind on the will of a divine creator—specifically the God of the Bible.

That's important because we have to understand that our rights—the rights of all human beings—are declared by America's founding document to be a direct descendent of the will of the living God.

God granted those rights, and government exists for the sole purpose of protecting those rights.

In the estimation of Thomas Jefferson, one of the founding fathers, the nation of the United States of America would not even exist except for the divine guidance and empowering of the living God.

That's important, because today, several words in the First Amendment of the U.S. Constitution are causing some problems:

Congress shall make no law respecting an establishment of religion, or prohibiting the free exercise thereof; or abridging the freedom of speech, or of the press; or the right of the people peaceably to assemble, and to petition the Government for a redress of grievances.

The bolded part of the First Amendment above is called the "establishment clause" of the amendment.

It essentially means the government may not establish a state religion or forbid anyone from exercising their religion.

The establishment part of that has been widely interpreted by courts in the nation as meaning that the

government cannot have any relationship with religion at all.
   In 1800, Republican Thomas Jefferson defeated Federalist John Adams in one of the most bitterly contested presidential elections in American history. The Federalists fiercely attacked Jefferson, questioning his religious beliefs and calling him an "infidel" and an "atheist." Some folks were so convinced of his heathenism that they buried family Bibles, fearing that Jefferson would confiscate and burn them when he became president. This distrust of Jefferson had been brewing for nearly 20 years, even though he had written several works in support of religious freedom.
   There were many, though, who were devoted to Jefferson. Among these were the fiercely loyal Republicans of the Danbury Baptist Association. They had written the president a somewhat belated letter, congratulating him on his election to office and applauding his lifelong devotion to religious liberty. On New Year's Day, 1802, Jefferson replied to this group.
   Because Jefferson's foes had vilified him as an infidel, he hoped this letter would reassure the pious Baptists that he was a friend of religion and an advocate of religious liberty. Jefferson also wanted to use the letter as a vehicle to explain his views on a politically divisive issue—why he, as president, had declined to proclaim days for public thanksgiving and prayer, as Presidents Washington and Adams had done before him.
   In his letter, Jefferson endorsed the Danbury Baptists' desire for religious freedom. Declaring that religion is a matter between a man and his God, Jefferson reaffirmed his commitment to the First Amendment. He noted that its establishment and free exercise clauses denied the government the authority to establish a religion or to dictate one's religious beliefs, "thus building a wall of separation between Church and State."
   That phrase, taken from that letter, has been bandied about again and again, and used as a window into the mind of Jefferson in legal rulings to determine exactly what the First Amendment was trying to say.
   The problem is that Jefferson's clear motive was to prohibit the government from forming and endorsing one church over

all others, as the monarchy in Great Britain had done.

It's clear from any, but the most atheistically biased perspective, that Jefferson did not intend to divest the government completely of any reference to God—especially since he was the guy who penned the words in the Declaration of Independence that said all the rights the government was instituted to protect were given to men by the living God!

> **Prayer Target Two**
> Lift up and exalt the Name of our Lord Creator, Governor of the Universe and Supreme Judge of the World, as He is referred to in many state constitutions and in the Declaration of Independence
>
> "O magnify the LORD with me, and let us exalt his name together" (Psalm 34:3).
>
> "Exalt ye the LORD our God, and worship at his footstool; for he is holy" (Psalm 99:5).

The forces of atheism in America have used the establishment clause to push prayer out of schools, remove crosses from public buildings and force religion completely out of public life.

They ignore simple facts like the Congress opening each session with prayer and the Supreme Court invoking God's wisdom before each session.

Instead, they focus on battles they can win—fighting the smaller foes like state governments.

Such was the case in Alabama.

Alabama Supreme Court Chief Justice Roy Moore, a believer, decided to take a stand.

Moore, who firmly believed that the foundation of law and government in America was the endowment of the living God to every man, woman and child on the planet, decided to acknowledge God and His influence in the law by placing a monument inside the Supreme Court: a stone engraving of the Ten Commandments.

No sooner had he placed the monument inside the court than the atheists went ballistic—how dare a government representative acknowledge God?

They immediately filed lawsuits, alleging that Moore's action violated the "separation of Church and state."

Now remember, partner, "separation of church and state" is not official government doctrine. It is an excerpt from a letter in which Thomas Jefferson is actually saying the government should not discriminate between religions.

The official government doctrine is that Congress can't make a law barring the practice of religion or instituting a state religion—forcing people to worship a certain way.

But those who are biased against Christianity don't care what the law actually **says**; they're interested in how they can interpret it to support their position.

So judicial activists have boxed in religion, slowly narrowing the walls on practice of religion and the boundaries in which it can be interpreted.

Judge Moore was suspended from his position as Chief Justice of the state of Alabama because he refused to remove the monument of the Ten Commandments at the behest of the federal government.

At this point, it's crucial to remember the United States is essentially a union of 50 countries that have agreed to work together in harmony, contributing for a common defense and large projects that the individual nations couldn't do by themselves.

The vision for the federal government is it would be small and limited, and most powers would be reserved for the states themselves.

Any powers not granted to the federal government explicitly were not implied and were given to the states.

But as the federal government has grown larger and more powerful, its limited status has diminished, superceded by a self-preserving method of taking whatever power it can.

So it demands the states comply with its directives, taking ultimate power.

Technically, since the federal government can't prohibit the free exercise of religion, it was unconstitutional for the federal government to tell a state Supreme Court Justice he couldn't exercise his belief in the God from whom our rights descend by displaying a monument to the base of the laws we're all required to follow.

Read the next chapter to understand why this problem is fundamental.

Prayer Target Three

Pray and ask forgiveness for the sins of our generation and the generations before us for not taking a godly stand when United States policies were enacted that violated the laws of God.

And I set my face unto the Lord God, to seek by prayer and supplications, with fasting, and sackcloth, and ashes: And I prayed unto the LORD my God, and made my confession, and said, O Lord, the great and dreadful God, keeping the covenant and mercy to them that love him, and to them that keep his commandments; We have sinned, and have committed iniquity, and have done wickedly, and have rebelled, even by departing from thy precepts and from thy judgments...To the Lord our God belong mercies and forgivenesses, though we have rebelled against him; Neither have we obeyed the voice of the LORD our God, to walk in his laws, which he set before us by his servants the prophets...therefore the curse is poured upon us, and the oath that is written in the law of Moses the servant of God, because we have sinned against him...As it is written in the law of Moses, all this evil is come upon us: yet made we not our prayer before the LORD our God, that we might turn from our iniquities, and understand thy truth.. Therefore hath the LORD watched upon the evil, and brought it upon us: for the LORD our God is righteous in all his works which he doeth: for we obeyed not his voice...O Lord, according to all thy righteousness, I beseech thee, let thine anger and thy fury be turned away...

Daniel 9:3-5, 9-10, 13-14 & 16

Chapter 2
Denying God and Persecuting Those Who Acknowledge Him

America was founded on the idea that the living God was in charge, and He was responsible for our rights as humans.

It was founded on the idea that a nation which denies Him can't long exist.

America was the first country, since the nation of Israel, which was founded on the idea that serving the living God was the reason the nation existed in the first place.

Even the form of government, a Democratic Republic, was designed around the idea that God governs, through anointed and appointed men and women, people who have given their consent to be governed in such a way.

But in the last 50 or so years, America has become increasingly secular, denying the God who gave us our rights, as well as, His protection and blessing on the nation.

Slowly but surely, America has pushed God out of His center place in our nation—even going so far as to ridicule a presidential candidate who said he prayed every day, and who said his biggest hero was Jesus Christ.

They actually had the gall to say that they would not vote for him because they were afraid he might govern based on his morality and his Christian convictions.

When people refuse to vote for a man because he has **morals**, the world is in a precarious position!

The goal of these secularizers is to make America into a completely godless nation—a nation that believes it exists because of the people, and not because of a God who gave them the rights they depend on to be a nation.

Their tactics in this attack are anything but civilized.

They don't focus on the debate and its facts; instead, they demonize and ridicule those who don't agree with their interpretation of the debate, and when that doesn't work, they employ the courts to reinterpret laws and impose federal power where the Constitution gives it no explicit jurisdiction.

By any means, the federal government should have no say in whether Judge Roy Moore can display a monument in his courtroom—Alabama, after all, is part of the United States by its own consent, and it has the right to reasonably expect the federal government to respect its jurisdiction as a state.

That, of course, is a quaint view, all but outdated for its idyllic view of the relationship between the states and the federal government. In theory, that's how it works, but in reality, the federal government has become all-powerful over the states, completely standing the Constitution on its ear.

At the root of the dispute is the federal government imposing a restriction originally intended to restrain Congressional power over the states!

It is a travesty of justice, but I fear this kind of intrusion will never stop and America is past the point of no return.

Understand, I'm not saying what will happen in the case of Judge Roy Moore; it's quite possible the U.S. Supreme Court will hear and reverse the lower court's decision, or they could leave it in place.

But the specific case is not what I'm talking about; I'm talking about the forces behind that specific case.

Even if Roy Moore is reinstated and allowed to keep his monument of the Ten Commandments, the forces of atheism will continue to chip away at our liberties until they have achieved their goal of making the United States a completely secular and atheistic nation.

To that end, they are prepared to persecute anyone who believes in God and is willing to act on that belief—even if he's the Chief Justice of a Supreme Court.

That persecution is not just an emotional reaction on their part—it is part of their tactics, a way of making dissenters afraid to vocalize their dissent. It's one of the methods they use to enact their atheistic agenda, and it will only get worse.

The day will come, Jesus said, when those who kill you will think they're doing God a service:
> *These things have I spoken unto you, that ye should not be offended. They shall put you out of the synagogues: yea, the time cometh, that whosoever killeth you will think that he doeth God service.* **And these things will they do unto you, because they have not known the Father, nor me.**
> John 16:1-3

The persecution of Christians will increase to unbelievable

Prayer Target Four
Pray the citizens and lawmakers will return to the godly roots of our great country and the original intent of the Constitution.

I exhort therefore, that, first of all, supplications, prayers, intercessions, and giving of thanks, be made for all men; For kings, and for all that are in authority; that we may lead a quiet and peaceable life in all godliness and honesty. For this is good and acceptable in the sight of God our Saviour; Who will have all men to be saved, and to come unto the knowledge of the truth.
I Timothy 2:1-4

---

proportions. I know many have proclaimed that Christians in America are even now persecuted, but that's because they have no true idea what persecution means—talk to pastors in Vietnam; then you'll know what persecution is.

What is called "persecution" in the United States is actually more like taunting. Even when churches have been fined and gotten in trouble for participating in political activities, it hasn't been "persecution" as much as it has been harassment.

Persecution is being jailed or killed for preaching the Gospel.

And it will come to that in America eventually—maybe even sooner than we realize.

Chapter 3

The Prophecy

> **Prayer Target Five**
> Pray that America will appoint godly judges according to the standards set forth in Exodus 18:21.
>
> Moreover thou shalt provide out of all the people able men, such as fear God, men of truth, hating covetousness; and place such over them, to be rulers of thousands, and rulers of hundreds, rulers of fifties, and rulers of tens.

God has given me a tremendous prophecy to deliver to you, something to prepare you for what is to come.

As I write this, it is late 2003. God spoke to me just as clearly as He ever has, and told me this: 2004 will be the most disastrous, problematic year in history for the United States of America.

Even now, we'll begin to see the hand of the enemy come into this nation as never before, and it will spread from America to the nations of the world.

America, you see, is a beacon for the rest of the world.

Much as the Statue of Liberty is a sign of hope for immigrants arriving in their new home, America itself is a leader, a lighthouse, for the rest of the world.

They look to America for everything.

They look to America for financial matters, for military matters, for political leadership, for policing, for solving the world's problems—and for one of its most recognizable exports: the Gospel of Jesus Christ.

America is the world leader in culture.

Let me say that again, because it's something you don't hear very often.

In fact, America is often called a land without culture, but that is absolutely not true.

America is a world leader in culture.

Go to almost any developing nation, and you'll see American culture everywhere; our buildings, our modes of dress, our haircuts, our money, our movies, our books, our Internet—even our language—is to be found all over the world.

American culture is like a blanket that has covered the entire world.

As something happens in America, it trickles down to the rest of the world, and they invariably embrace it.

As America turns against God and the hand of the enemy strengthens here, that flip-flop will trickle down to the rest of the world, poisoning it with the evil that results from it.

So I repeat again: **2004 will be the most problematic year in history for the United States.**

Remember, all truth is parallel.

What happens in the natural is a reflection of what is happening in the spiritual.

> *For if he were on earth, he should not be a priest, seeing that there are priests that offer gifts according to the law: Who serve unto the example and shadow of heavenly things, as Moses was admonished of God when he was about to make the tabernacle: for, See, saith he, that thou make all things according to the pattern shown to thee in the mount.*
>
> Hebrews 8:4-5

What Moses saw and implemented as the Law was a physical reflection of what he had seen in the spiritual.

All truth is parallel.

What will happen in America during 2004 will happen in the natural, because it will be a reflection of what is happening in the spiritual.

The natural reasons are easy to figure out:

- 2004 is an election year, during which the enemies of America will attempt to influence the election by increasing terrorism, thereby portraying the current administration (and its anti-terrorism crusade) as weak and wrong-headed.
- Politicians and those in high places are self-proclaimed Christians who loudly and openly proclaim

their faith in the living God and his Son, Jesus Christ but fail to uphold His teachings.

Those two things are parallels of the spiritual; there is political change afoot, which is a reflection of the war that is going on in the spiritual—a war against your soul, and against your calling to reach out to the lost.

Tangentially related is the politicians and high-level officials who proclaim God; their positions put them in a

---

Prayer Target Six

Pray for the wisdom of God to permeate all Supreme Court decisions.

Ye shall do no unrighteousness in judgment: thou shalt not respect the person of the poor, nor honour the person of the mighty: but in righteousness shalt thou judge thy neighbour.

Leviticus 19:15

"And said to the judges, Take heed what ye do: for ye judge not for man, but for the LORD, who is with you in the judgment" (II Chronicles 19:6).

---

place to facilitate the smoother preaching of the Gospel.

In the coming year, we will begin to see upheavals in the country.

We will see terrorist acts all over the country—they may not be of the grand scale as the September 11 attacks, but they will pop up all over the place.

Remember the huge blackout that hit New York earlier in 2003? The government wouldn't tell you even if they had evidence that it was caused by a terrorist act.

Now, understand, I'm not saying it was caused by a terrorist act; I'm saying if it had been, the government wouldn't tell you because that would incite a tremendous panic all over the nation. If terrorists can strike when and where they want and have such a profound impact, nobody is safe.

Terrorists **can** strike when and wherever they want. There's not much the government can do to protect you.

Though terrorists may not have caused the New York blackout, it's entirely conceivable that they **could**.

And that frightens the government, so they stay quiet about it and try to keep the public calm by glossing over the problem.

The fact is, terrorism is coming. It will strike here, and it will be of a greater scale and pervasiveness than anyone could ever have predicted.

America will go through upheaval like it never has before in history. We will see natural disasters, hurricanes, tornadoes, fires and floods like never before.

That time is coming.

Prophecy is given to prepare you, not scare you.

God wants you to know what's coming so you can prepare and be ready when it does.

And God has also, with the prophecy, shown me how you can prepare for it! I will share that with you in Chapter five of this book.

Chapter 4

How the Mighty Have Fallen

Terrorism, unrest and persecution of Christians are ONLY THE BEGINNING!

I believe God wants me to reveal to you what I have previously only told a chosen few close ministry associates–a prophecy of such incredible scope and power that it literally may leave you shaking!

God gives us prophecy for a specific reason...The nature of foretelling prophecy is to see into the future and reveal events to come that may not always be pleasant...

Think of the example of the prophet Jonah; he was called to give a specific and terrifying message to the people of the Assyrian capital of Ninevah:

> Arise, go unto Nineveh, that great city, and preach unto it the preaching that I bid thee. So Jonah arose, and went unto Nineveh, according to the word of the LORD. Now Nineveh was an exceeding great city of three days' journey. And Jonah began to enter into the city a day's journey, and he cried, and said, a **Yet forty days, and Nineveh shall be overthrown.**
>
> Jonah 3:2-4

Now, there was nothing pleasant about Jonah's prophecy!

In fact, I've found that many Christians assume Jonah preached repentance to the Ninevites—but he did no such thing! All he told them was that judgment was coming their way, and their city had only 40 days of freedom left!

But just as clear as it is that God did not instruct the prophet to **preach** repentance; repentance **is** what God wanted to see!

The prophecy, though negative, was not intended to **scare** the people of Ninevah. It was intended to **prepare** them.

And that's what God still does with prophecy today—He uses

it not to scare you, but to prepare you for what is to come.

God has given me a special mandate to hear from Him and to report it to you—no matter what He says.

In the forward of this book I shared what God spoke to me in the beginning of the 1990's. God awoke me out of a deep sleep to reveal to me five waves of the Holy Spirit coming in the 1990's and five crises that would strike during the same time.

When I was given this message, the world was in the middle of one of the strongest and most prosperous economies in history! Everyone was getting richer, and everyone was loving life!

But one of the crises God had me prophesy was that a financial dearth would sweep the world and prosperity would melt away into poverty.

Let me tell you, when I delivered that message, people **laughed** at me. They said I was crazy or I had lost it.

But I stuck by my guns, because after 57 years in the ministry, I can only do what I have been doing all along—trust God, even when what He's doing seems completely foreign to me.

So I prophesied the five crises, and EVERY ONE OF THEM CAME TRUE!

Time and time again, God has proven that He is a God who speaks to people today—He is a God who is intimately interested in our affairs, and who wants us to know what He's doing!

"Surely the Lord GOD will do nothing, but he revealeth his secret unto his servants the prophets" (Amos 3:7).

When God has a plan, He reveals that plan to His servants, the prophets, because He wants his people to KNOW what He's doing before He does it! He doesn't want it to come as a surprise.

That's why, in early 1990, God revealed to me the five waves and five crises that were to come in the 1990s, and that's why He has revealed this tremendous prophecy to me now.

Trouble Ahead for America

This may offend some, but 2003 has been a gay year in America. We've had laws against sodomy overturned by the Supreme Court, an openly gay bishop being recognized in a mainstream church and gay marriages recognized in our neighbor to the north, Canada.

But those are peripheral issues—gay bishops in the church are an issue to be worked out in a doctrinal way, something that the church in which it is a problem will need to deal with through prayer and communion with God.

But a worse thing happened during 2003—something that gave an indication in an official way that the country wants nothing more to do with God, the removal of the Ten Commandments monument I spoke about in Chapter two. Please bear with me as I reemphasize the issue again here.

Alabama Supreme Court Chief Justice Roy Moore has a simple belief; he believes that America was founded on the Bible and that our system of laws is based on the legal system set up under the administration of Moses—specifically the Ten Commandments.

As such, Moore set up a monument to the founding documents of the American legal system in the foyer of the Alabama Supreme Court—he had a two-ton stone carving of the Ten Commandments placed there.

And the fireworks started.

Civil libertarians came out of the woodwork, filing lawsuits saying Moore's display violated their rights and trampled on the "separation of church and state" they believe is implied by the Constitution's First Amendment clause against Congress establishing a formal religion.

The lawsuit resulted in an order for Moore to remove the monument, but he stuck by his guns—his contention is clear: the Constitution of the state of Alabama acknowledges God, and his oath requires him to acknowledge God. The Declaration of Independence states that Americans' rights come directly from God, and if he can't acknowledge God because of judges' orders, the judges are breaking the law that requires him to acknowledge God.

His point did not sit well with a federal judge, who suspended Moore from the bench pending an appeal, which as of this writing, Moore has filed with the U.S. Supreme Court. The case has a tremendous prophetic impact on the coming years.

This case simply makes the point that God wanted me to prophesy to you:

> **Prayer Target Seven**
> **Pray that all laws on the books that do not honor God and the Bible would be reversed or removed.**
>
> **Now therefore hearken, O Israel, unto the statutes and unto the judgments, which I teach you, for to do them, that ye may live, and go in and possess the land which the LORD God of your fathers giveth you. Ye shall not add unto the word which I command you, neither shall ye diminish ought from it, that ye may keep the commandments of the LORD your God which I command you.**
>
> **Deuteronomy 4:1-2**

2004 will be the most problematic year for the United States of America. Next year, we'll begin to see the hand of the enemy come into this nation as never before, and it will spread from America to the nations of the world.

It's an election year in America, and the enemy will stir up the people in this country against God's forces as never before. The enemy is angry—no, he's FURIOUS—because people are in political areas of the world claiming to know Jesus Christ and trying to serve Him in prayer.

Right now, we have a Christian in the White House, and forces are coming against him from all directions in unprecedented ways.

> **Prayer Target Eight**
> **Pray that those in authority over us will walk in the ways of the Lord, and stand on the side of justice and judgment.**
>
> **"The king's heart is in the hand of the LORD, as the rivers of water: he turneth it whithersoever he will. To do justice and judgment is more acceptable to the LORD than sacrifice" (Proverbs 21:1 & 3).**

Judge Roy Moore is a Bible-believing Christian, and the forces are coming against him in incredible intensity.

The rationale for these forces is probably political, but we know the true battle is spiritual—they may not even understand why they are acting the way they are; but we know spiritual forces are behind their dissimulation.

God told me to prophesy that we're going to begin to see churning and unrest in this country. We will see terrorist acts all over the United States of America to try to cause disruption and unrest—the attacks of September 11, 2001 were simply the harbingers of more terrorism to come. The terrorists ARE NOT DONE YET.

What is Next?

We will begin to mobilize a mighty Prayer initiative with people all over the country and the world—a prayer force focused on one thing: undoing the wrong the devil is doing in the world.

If my people, which are called by my name, shall humble themselves, and pray, and seek my face, and turn from their wicked ways; then will I hear from heaven, and will forgive their sin, and will heal their land.

2 Chronicles 7:14

It's not just a slogan when we say "greater is He who is in us than he who is in the world."

When God is for us, who can be against us? Christians are not some milquetoast wimps sitting around watching the world happen to them—we are blood-bought, Spirit-filled, armed to the teeth with the Word of God and unafraid of any devil that dares to stand in our way! We shouldn't be fearing the forces of darkness in the world—they should be fearing **us**!

God has revealed to me that there has got to be a spirit of repentance that will sweep across this nation. It will never happen by preaching, nor by the eloquent words spoken from countless pulpits across the land.

It will happen when we can get together and mobilize the body of Christ to pray as never before!

Did you get that?

God will move when Christians have gotten together to **ask** Him to move! During the day of Jonah, God sent a warning to Ninevah, and the people there, in one accord, ripped their clothes and put ashes on their heads, repenting earnestly for the evils they had wrought.

They started a religious revival that lasted for **100 years**! Their unity in turning to God was on a level we have never seen in our age, but I believe it's something we're going to see before the return of Christ.

We are going on the offensive!

We're going to mobilize hundreds of churches. Right after the World Conference, I'm calling for seven days of prayer and fasting. This appeal will be released in all the major magazines and newspapers around the country and inside churches!

We will have daily prayer meetings in the World Prayer Center broadcast over the internet. Monthly prayer meetings will be broadcast over Television and the internet.

Our intent is to mobilize all Christians of all faiths to band together and change the direction of our great nation from godlessness to godliness.

This is not a one-man job. I can't call for prayer and fasting and expect to get results. It has to be a grassroots movement, where people all over the nation are coming to God and moving in unison with other Christians all over the nation!

We have to mobilize the Body of Christ. Sound an alarm on the holy mountain of Almighty God like Joel!

The alarm is this: the devil has declared war on Christianity in America, but we stand firm and strong to tell him in no uncertain terms, **HE CAN'T HAVE IT!**

You can tear down the monument in Alabama, but you can't destroy the Ten Commandments. They are not a monument of stone! They are the Word of the living God, written on the hearts of the people of Almighty God!

The stone monument the devil has succeeded in removing is nothing but a shadow. An imperfect representation of the God who inspired it.

The true power of God is found in the hearts of His people!

Chapter 5
What You Can Do NOW

> **Prayer Target Nine**
> Pray that our Governors, Senators, Congress, House of Representatives, Supreme Court Judges will walk in the ways of the Lord, and stand on the side of justice and judgment.
>
> The king's heart is in the hand of the LORD, as the rivers of water: he turneth it whithersoever he will. To do justice and judgment is more acceptable to the LORD than sacrifice.
> Proverbs 21:1 & 3

Verily I say unto you, Whatsoever ye shall bind on earth shall be bound in heaven: and whatsoever ye shall loose on earth shall be loosed in heaven. Again I say unto you, That if two of you shall agree on earth as touching any thing that they shall ask, it shall be done for them of my Father which is in heaven. For where two or three are gathered together in my name, there am I in the midst of them. Matthew 18:18-20

God has called us to be praying people.

When the people of Israel had sinned against God, He said this to Moses:

And the LORD said unto Moses, I have seen this people, and, behold, it is a stiffnecked people: Now therefore let me alone, that my wrath may wax hot against them, and that **I may consume them: and I will make of thee a great nation..**
Exodus 32:9-10

In this passage God is telling His prophet what He is about to do. He tells Moses to hang back so He can go destroy all the people of Israel—it is a prophecy of what

He is going to do.

But God is not an angry and vengeful God by nature. He is slow to wrath and quick to forgive!

Moses, understanding the nature of God, did not settle for the doom that was prophesied!

Instead, the prophet of God said this:

And Moses besought the LORD his God, and said, LORD, why doth thy wrath wax hot against thy people, which thou hast brought forth out of the land of Egypt with great power, and with a mighty hand? Wherefore should the Egyptians speak, and say, For mischief did he bring them out, to slay them in the mountains, and to consume them from the face of the earth? Turn from thy fierce wrath, and repent of this evil against thy people. Remember Abraham, Isaac, and Israel, thy servants, to whom thou swarest by thine own self, and saidst unto them, I will multiply your seed as the stars of heaven, and all this land that I have spoken of will I give unto your seed, and they shall inherit it for ever.

Exodus 32:11-13

What was Moses' secret weapon? Moses **PRAYED!**

He talked to God and asked God to reconsider, to not do what He had prophesied He would do.

After that, the Bible says God **CHANGED HIS MIND**!

He instead showered Israel with GRACE!

God has called us to do as Moses did—He has told us what He is about to do, but He has called us to PRAY!

There has to be a spirit of repentance that will sweep across this nation. It will never happen by preaching. It will happen when we can get together and mobilize the body of Christ to pray as never before!

Prayer Target Ten

Pray for all members in the Body of Christ, that they would return to righteousness and mercy.

"He that followeth after righteousness and mercy findeth life, righteousness, and honor" (Proverbs 21:21).

"For I am the LORD that bringeth you up out of the land of Egypt, to be your God: ye shall therefore be holy, for I am holy" (Leviticus 11:45).

We are going to stand in the gap and pray to the living God to bring salvation on this nation as never before! To send out the Gospel of Jesus Christ from this place as never before!

Friend, together, we can make a tremendous change in the world together!

SAVE AMERICA NOW!

Epilogue:
God's servant speaks

I want to be clear about one thing here: God has given me a specific and dynamic message to communicate to the body of Christ.

I've already covered this prophecy in this book, but I wanted to break it out in a specific way to emphasize the importance of it — the sheer magnitude of it.

That means it needs its own section.

God recently spoke to me in an incredible way. He said to me, "Son, mobilize the Body of Christ, because next year will be the most problematic year in the history of the United States."

In 2004, we will begin to see the hand of the enemy come into this nation as never before.

It will spread from America to other nations of the world.

The problems will be in every arena, from political to terrorism to financial and sociological. Not all will happen at one time, and not all will blanket every person.

There are several reasons that can be cited in the natural to explain what will be coming in the next few days.

First, it's an election year, and the enemy will stir the country against those who stand for God in a way that has never before been seen.

Many people in places of elected office are openly claiming Jesus Christ as their Lord — not just in a political way as has happened so often in the past, but they are actively petitioning God for guidance in the way they fulfill their offices.

The devil is mad.

I'm not saying this to try to scare you, but to prepare you. We will see upheavals in this country because of the presence of Christians in places of power, and for other reasons.

For instance, terrorism will increase in this nation both for revenge over American actions in the Middle East and to try to disrupt the political process and guide it to a conclusion that is acceptable to those propagating the terrorism.

If the government knew a disruption in the nation was terrorism, it seems likely to me that they'd seek to keep that connection silent to avoid mass panic.

It's only wise on their part. People fearing terrorism do crazy things. But watch in the year 2004 — many disruptions will happen, many of them will likely be terrorism, though the governments and complicit media may try to keep that fact quiet.

But through all these upheavals and trouble, God is still in control!

God is still moving His people, and He is still taking that which was intended for evil and turning it into good for His people who love Him.

In the midst of all this trouble, God will raise up His people to greater power, higher heights and more awesome depth in Him!

Starting in January, I called for seven days of prayer and fasting for the nation, kicking off our drive to SAVE AMERICA NOW!

As part of the outreach, we are still calling on churches and Christians all over America to get on their knees with us and PRAY and INTERCEDE for the salvation of America from the degraded position it now finds itself in.

Only through PRAYER and FASTING can we hope to call this nation back to God!

This is not just a one-man job! We have to mobilize the body of Christ as Joel did, sounding an alarm on the holy mountain of God almighty!

Even more, we are planning to continue blitzing America with prime time television specials, church mobilizations, full-page ads in all the major newspapers in the nation, magazine ads, television and radio ads and more!

Friends,—will you join me in this Prayer Anointing to Save America Now.

1) Join the Prayer Anointing by signing a commitment. Be on record to pray.
2) Share this booklet with a friend. Send for more copies to distribute.
3) Send a Save America Now gift to help me launch the greatest Prayer Anointing the world has ever seen.

Please pray about joining us now by filling out the form.

Chairman of the Save America Now!
Board of Reference

SAVE AMERICA NOW!

Miracles Happen When Someone Cares... And We Care What Happens To You!

Call if you need healing, restoration in your marriage, financial breakthrough, deliverance from alcohol, drugs or other addictions.

WORLD PRAYER CENTER

P
R

- Prayer Help Line

A

- Trained, anointed intercessors. Only qualified, trained intercessors will be on the phone lines

YOUR PHONE IS YOUR POINT OF CONTACT!

- Non-denominational: We encourage Catholic, Protestants, Jews, people of all faiths to call

Y

You Never Have To Face Your Circumstances Alone!

E

There is no distance in prayer!

Our trained intercessors are ready to pray and believe God for the miracle you need!

R

Call the Morris Cerullo Prayer Help Line

1-858-HELPLINE
435-7546

helpline@mcwe.com
Fax: 858-427-0555

34

❑ I am standing with you. I agree we have to change the moral direction of America. We have to pray that God will SAVE AMERICA NOW!

❑ I will pray.

❑ Enclosed is an offering to help with the cost of the *SAVE AMERICA NOW!* campaign $£ _____.

Name _____

Address _____

City _____ State or Province _____

Postal Code _____ Phone Number (___)_____

E-mail _____

Fax _____

Mail today to:

SAVE AMERICA NOW!

San Diego: P.O. Box 85260 • San Diego, CA 92186-5260

Web site: www.save-america-now.com

Email: contact@save-america-now.com

For prayer, call: **1-858-HELPLINE**
435-7546

Save America Now!